ALL AROUND THE WORLD
RUSSIA

by Jessica Dean

po go

Ideas for Parents and Teachers

Pogo Books let children practice reading informational text while introducing them to nonfiction features such as headings, labels, sidebars, maps, and diagrams, as well as a table of contents, glossary, and index.

Carefully leveled text with a strong photo match offers early fluent readers the support they need to succeed.

Before Reading

- "Walk" through the book and point out the various nonfiction features. Ask the student what purpose each feature serves.
- Look at the glossary together. Read and discuss the words.

Read the Book

- Have the child read the book independently.
- Invite him or her to list questions that arise from reading.

After Reading

- Discuss the child's questions. Talk about how he or she might find answers to those questions.
- Prompt the child to think more. Ask: The czars brought beautiful art and style to Russia. The next leaders thought machines and labor were better. What do you think is better?

Pogo Books are published by Jump!
5357 Penn Avenue South
Minneapolis, MN 55419
www.jumplibrary.com

Library of Congress Cataloging-in-Publication Data

Names: Dean, Jessica, 1963- author.
Title: Russia / by Jessica Dean.
Description: Minneapolis, MN : Jump!, Inc., 2018.
Series: All around the world | Includes bibliographical references and index.
Identifiers: LCCN 2017061529 (print)
LCCN 2018001182 (ebook) | ISBN 9781624969249 (ebook)
ISBN 9781624969225 (hardcover : alk. paper)
ISBN 9781624969232 (pbk.)
Subjects: LCSH: Russia (Federation) —Juvenile literature.
Classification: LCC DK510.23 (ebook) | LCC DK510.23 .D43 2019 (print) | DDC 947—dc23
LC record available at https://lccn.loc.gov/2017061529

Editor: Kristine Spanier
Book Designer: Leah Sanders

Photo Credits: finallast/Shutterstock, cover; Danweits/Shutterstock, 1; Pixfiction/Shutterstock, 3; Mikhail Olykainen/Shutterstock, 4; Mordoiff/iStock, 5; yulenochekk/iStock, 6-7; FloridaStock/Shutterstock, 8-9; Danita Delimont/Getty, 10-11; Easyturn/iStock, 12; Fedor Sidorov/Shutterstock, 13; Popova Valeriya/Shutterstock, 14-15; df028/Shutterstock, 16-17; gkrphoto/iStock, 18; A. Zhuravleva/Shutterstock, 19; Evgeniy Kalinovskiy/Shutterstock, 20-21; AdaCo/Shutterstock, 23.

Printed in the United States of America at Corporate Graphics in North Mankato, Minnesota.

TABLE OF CONTENTS

CHAPTER 1

· ·

WELCOME TO RUSSIA!

Would you like to play with wooden nesting dolls? Want to go where the sun never sets? How does a bowl of pink soup sound? Let's explore Russia!

Russia was once ruled by kings called **czars**. They built grand **palaces** and beautiful cities. Many buildings have onion-shaped domes. Magnificent art is found nearly everywhere.

Moscow is the **capital**. The Kremlin is the **seat** of the government. The president lives here. He runs the country. The **prime minister** helps. So does the **duma**. This is a group of lawmakers.

The Red Square is in Moscow, too. It is one of the largest town squares in the world. St. Basil's Cathedral is here.

WHAT DO YOU THINK?

Many leaders here have been controversial. Statues of these leaders are located throughout the country. Do you think they should be removed? Why or why not?

St. Basil's Cathedral

Siberia is located in the north. This **province** is filled with vast **natural resources**. Like what? Coal. Petroleum. Natural gas. Gold.

Winters here are severe. Temperatures can drop to -90° Fahrenheit (-68° Celsius). Polar bears fish in the Arctic Ocean nearby.

DID YOU KNOW?

The Trans-Siberian Railway runs through Siberia. It is the longest single rail system in the world. How long is it? Almost 6,000 miles (9,660 kilometers)! It was finished in 1916. It runs from Moscow to Vladivostok.

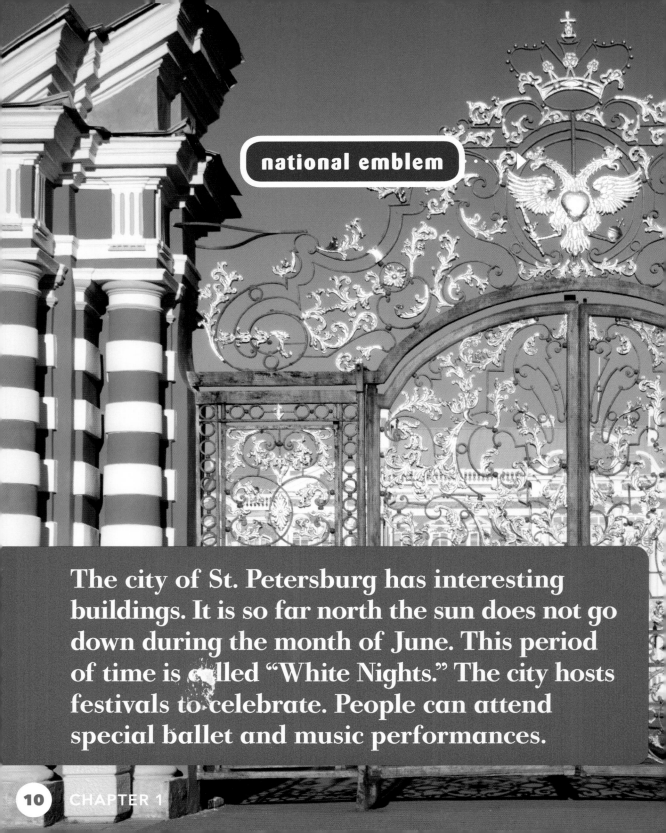

national emblem

The city of St. Petersburg has interesting buildings. It is so far north the sun does not go down during the month of June. This period of time is called "White Nights." The city hosts festivals to celebrate. People can attend special ballet and music performances.

TAKE A LOOK!

The national **emblem** is found all over Russia. The **modern** design is based on one from more than 500 years ago. Each element has special meaning.

1. three crowns: relationship between Russia, Ukraine, and Belarus
2. two heads: equal importance of European and Asian continents
3. scepter: power
4. orb: authority

CHAPTER 2

LIFE IN RUSSIA

Most Russians now live in modern cities. Families may live in small apartments. Grandparents might share the space, too.

Some still live on farms. They grow grain. What else? Sugar beets. Fruits. Vegetables.

Many Russians work with computers. Or in science. Some work for companies that make gas. Others have **service jobs**.

To get to work, people walk or take the **subway**. Some subway stations are grand spaces filled with art.

subway

After work, people might hike or ski. Others go to plays, concerts, or the ballet. Some of the best ballet dancers in the world live here.

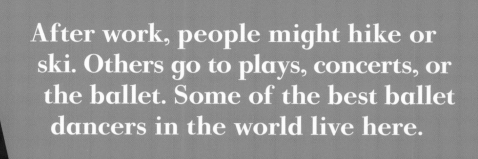

WHAT DO YOU THINK?

Why do you think hiking and skiing are popular activities in Russia? What outdoor activities are popular where you live?

CHAPTER 3

MEALS AND CELEBRATIONS

Russian food is simple and filling. A pink soup called borscht is made from beets.

borscht

dumplings

Hot cereal starts the day. It is made with grains. Lunch or dinner might be potato dumplings filled with meat. They are served with cabbage and dark rye bread.

Russia's oldest holiday is Maslenitsa. It celebrates the coming of spring. People dress up. They play tricks on each other. They eat blini. These are thin pancakes.

New Year's Day is the biggest holiday here. People decorate trees. Children receive presents.

There is so much to do here. What would you like to do in Russia?

blini

QUICK FACTS & TOOLS

RUSSIA

Location: Europe and Asia

Size: 6.6 million square miles (17.1 million square kilometers)

Population: 142,257,519 (July 2017 estimate)

Capital: Moscow

Type of Government: semi-presidential federation

Language: Russian

Exports: petroleum products, natural gas, metals, wood

GLOSSARY

capital: A city where government leaders meet.

czars: Emperors of Russia before the revolution of 1917.

duma: The representative council in Russia.

emblem: A symbol or a sign that represents something.

modern: Having to do with the present or recent times.

natural resources: Materials produced by the earth that are necessary or useful to people.

palaces: Large, fancy homes for rulers.

prime minister: The leader of a country.

province: A district or a region in a country.

seat: The central location of the government.

service jobs: Jobs and work that provide services for others, such as hotel, restaurant, and retail positions.

subway: A train that runs on underground tracks.

INDEX

TO LEARN MORE

Learning more is as easy as 1, 2, 3.

1) Go to www.factsurfer.com

2) Enter "Russia" into the search box.

3) Click the "Surf" button to see a list of websites.

With factsurfer, finding more information is just a click away.